A Little Child and God

My name

A Little Child and God

By Mary M. Landis
Illustrated by Edith Burkholder

Rod and Staff Publishers, Inc.
P.O. Box 3, Hwy. 172
Crockett, Kentucky 41413
Telephone: (606) 522-4348

Copyright 2006
Rod and Staff Publishers, Inc.
Crockett, Kentucky 41413

Printed in U.S.A.

ISBN 0-7399-2365-X
Catalog no. 2288

For my
Great-grandchildren

"Suffer the little children
to come unto me,
and forbid them not:
for of such is the kingdom of God"
(Mark 10:14).

"A little child shall lead them"
(Isaiah 11:6).

Our Father,
God,
who lives above,
Loves
children
with a tender love.

He's far away—
and yet He's near.

He speaks,
but not in words I hear.

But God sees me, and hears me too,
And watches all the things I do.

To this great God I'll pray today,
And these will be the words I'll say:

You saw me in the dark last night;
The moon—it was not shining bright.

I did not need
to be afraid,
Because I knew
the night You made.
And You could see me
plain and clear,
Were standing by me
very near.

And while I slept all snug and warm,
You kept me safely from all harm.

You woke me up
with light You sent—
I don't know where the darkness went—

But when the sun came up today,
The night had gone far, far away.

My morning prayer to God will be:
"Thank You for taking care of me.
In Jesus' Name. Amen."

I dressed in clothes You gave to me;

My breakfast also came from Thee.

So did my father and my mother,

My sister, and my baby brother.

My toy truck, and

My wagon too,
I know, dear God, are gifts from You;

My dish and spoon,

My chair and ball,
And ears to hear my mother's call.

My eyes see lovely things You made,
The flowers blooming in the shade,

The tree where Father made a swing,

The birds and sky and everything.

"These blessings, Lord,
I thank Thee for;
You give them all—
and many more.
And, God, take care
of me today
When I run out-of-doors
to play.
In Jesus' Name. Amen."

I laughed and ran

And sang

And played;

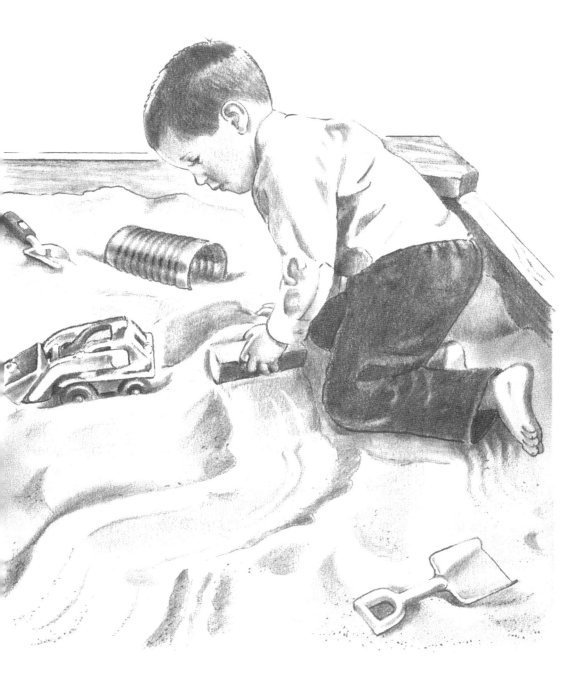

And in the sandbox, roads I made
That curved,

And had a bridge

And hill;

I stayed right there and played, until
My mother called me in to eat

And take a nap, so I'd be sweet.

When Father came,

He took my hand,

And we walked back across our land

Until we came to Grandpa's stile;

Then we sat down to rest awhile.

We talked about the things that grow—
How some grow fast and some grow slow.

Some things are giants, like a tree,

While tiny ants are hard to see.

He told me that the wind that blew,
The earth and sky were made by You.

You made the little bugs and things,

That crawl,

Or jump,

Or fly with wings.

And all the birds that fly and sing—
That You, dear God, made everything!

My father said that You made me
The way You planned for me to be—
My smile, my skin, my hair and eyes,

And that You even planned the size
That I would be when I'm a man.
He said I'm part of Your good plan.

Then Father took me on his knee,
And bowed his head and prayed for me;
That I would serve God all my days,
And follow Him in all my ways.

I like when Father
prays for me.
When I am big,
I want to be
Just like my father—
he loves You,
And I know that
I love You too.

We saw some dark clouds in the sky
And then a flash of lightning high;
And after that, the thunder came—
We knew that it was going to rain.

While we ran to the house together,
My father said, "God made the weather."

At night I prayed—these words I said
Before I tumbled into bed:

"Dear God, please hear
this thank-you prayer.
Today You kept
me in Your care.
Please bless my father
and my mother,
My sister, and
my baby brother.